RHYTHM IN MUSIC

A Text-Book

By

GEORGE A. WEDGE

G. SCHIRMER
(INCORPORATED)
NEW YORK

Copyright, 1927, by G. Schirmer, Inc.
33296

Printed in the U. S. A.

To
GASTON M. DETHIER

FOREWORD

This book aims to clear up the mystery surrounding the subject of rhythm in music. Rhythm, the most vital factor in all arts which depend upon the aural sense, must of necessity have a simple physical foundation. This physical element is inherent in all normal human beings and upon this basis artistic creation is developed.

With an understanding of its fundamental principles and a logical system of study correlative with the development of muscular technique there can be no excuse for unrhythmic musical performances.

Herein are given suggestions for developing and keeping a strict pulse and the performances of rhythms. The use of these elements made by composers in expressing their ideas and the application of this in interpretation will be considered in a later volume.

G. A. WEDGE.

New York.

TABLE OF CONTENTS

	PAGE
THE THEORY OF RHYTHM..	1

    1. Rhythm in Interpretation.
    2. Terminology.
    3. Pupils and Rhythm.

DRILLS FOR THE STUDY OF METER:
    I. Duple Meter, Beginning with the Accented Pulse........... 10
    II. Duple Meter, Beginning with the Unaccented Pulse......... 12
    III. Triple Meter, Beginning with the Accented Pulse........... 13
    IV. Triple Meter, Beginning with the Third Pulse............... 14
    V. Triple Meter, Beginning with the Second Pulse.............. 15
    VI. Quadruple Meter, Beginning with the Accented Pulse....... 16
    VII. Quadruple Meter, Beginning with the Fourth Pulse......... 18
    VIII. Quadruple Meter, Beginning with the Third Pulse.......... 19
    IX. Quadruple Meter, Beginning with the Second Pulse......... 20

DRILLS FOR THE STUDY OF RHYTHM:
    X. Added Pulses and Rests in Duple Meter..................... 21
    XI. Added Pulses in Triple Meter (the ♩.)...................... 22
    XII. Added Pulses in Triple Meter (the ♩ ♪): 3/4............... 24
    XIII. Quadruple Meter (the ♩)................................... 25
    XIV. Quadruple Meter (the ♩.).................................. 27

DRILLS FOR THE SUBDIVISION OF PULSES:
    XV. The Subdivision into Two................................... 28
    XVI. The Subdivision into Four.................................. 30
    XVII. The Subdivision into Three................................. 32
    XVIII. The Addition of Pulses in 6/8 (♩. and ♩ ♪) Time......... 34
    XIX. The ♩. and ♩ ♪ in 9/8 Time.............................. 35
    XX. The ♩. and ♩ ♪ in 12/8 Time............................. 36
    XXI. The Subdivision into Six................................... 36
    XXII. The ♩ ♫ in 6/8 Time..................................... 37
    XXIII. The ♫ in Duple Meter................................... 38

		PAGE
THE COMBINATION OF ADDED AND DIVIDED PULSES:		
XXIV.	Two-, Three- and Four-Pulse Meter	38
XXV.	Rhythms Formed by Using a Dot	41
XXVI.	The ♩.♪	42
XXVII.	The ♩.♫ in 6/8 Time	43
XXVIII.	The ♩.♬ in 6/8 Time	44
XXIX.	Thirty-Second Notes	45
THE TIE:		
XXX.	The Tie in Two-Pulse Meter	46
XXXI.	The Tie in Three- and Four-Pulse Meter	47
XXXII.	The Tie in 6/8 Time	48
IRREGULAR RHYTHMS:		
XXXIII.	Irregular Rhythms in Two-, Three-, Four- and Six-Pulse Meter	49
SYNCOPATED RHYTHMS:		
XXXIV.	Syncopated Rhythm in Two-, Three- and Four-Pulse Meter	50
XXXV.	Syncopated Rhythm in 6/8 Time	51
CROSS RHYTHMS:		
XXXVI.	Two against Three	52
XXXVII.	Three against Four	53

		PAGE
	THE COMBINATION OF ACCENT AND DIVIDED PULSES:	
XXIV.	Two-, Three- and Four-Pulse Meter	37
XXV.	Rhythms formed by Using a Part	41
XXVI.	The ![symbol]	43
XXVII.	The ![symbol] in 6/8 time	44
XXVIII.	The ![symbol] in 6/8 time	45
XXIX.	Thirty-second Notes	45

THE UNLIKE TREATMENT OF METERS:
XXX.	The Unlike Treatment of Meters	47
XXXI.	The Two-, Three- and Four-Pulse Meters	47
XXXII.	The 6/8 Time	48

IRREGULAR RHYTHMS:
| XXXIII. | Irregular Rhythms in Two-, Three- and Six-Pulse Meter | 49 |

SYNCOPATED RHYTHMS:
| XXXIV. | Syncopated Rhythm in Two-, Three- and Four-Pulse Meter | 50 |
| XXXV. | Syncopated Rhythm in 6/8 Time | 51 |

CROSS RHYTHMS:
| XXXVI. | Two against Three | 52 |
| XXXVII. | Three against Four | 53 |

RHYTHM IN MUSIC
THE THEORY OF RHYTHM

RHYTHM IN INTERPRETATION

Criticisms and discussions of concerts are generally concentrated upon the individual interpretations or readings of the compositions by the performers and conductors. Because programs are made up of compositions which are well known to the listeners, misunderstandings often occur on the part of the musically uneducated public, who are led to consider only the performer and not the composition. This is harmful to the young music student, as he is made to believe that it is necessary to "do something" to a composition before it can be understood. It causes interpreters in all branches of the art to exaggerate in tempi, to bring out hidden melodies which they imagine exist, and in some instances even to rewrite or rescore the composition. One might ask whether the composer does not make his wishes clear, or if the composition cannot stand on its own merits.

Symbols for musical sounds and methods for indicating the composer's wishes are somewhat inadequate. There seems to be little definite information about or consistency in the method of writing music. The great composers were often careless in writing, and in many cases their works have been so edited and changed that they would have difficulty in recognizing them.

Music is in many ways more personal than the other arts. It is difficult to say that a combination of sounds or a rhythm must express the same emotion to all auditors, or that the symbols upon the printed page must give the performer the thought of the composer and cause him, through the medium of his chosen instrument, to transmit the same thought to the audience. There is every possibility that the composer has one meaning, the performer another, and each auditor still another. But there are a few laws and scientific facts deduced from the works of great composers which can help the music student to approach more nearly the wishes of the composer and project these to the audience.

Many elements enter into the successful performance of a composition. The strongest of these is the time or pulse. This is the common bond between performer and auditor and the means of holding attention. Any psychologist will confirm the fact that most humans have inherent in their beings the fundamentals of the two basic factors that go to make up a musical composition, i. e., pitch and pulse. With the musically uneducated the latter is more important, since the first requisite of a performance is that the performer keep time, the musical sounds making little difference. In spite of the beauty of the slow movement of a symphony, one must accede a preference for the exhilaration of the marked pulse of an *allegro*. The appeal of so-called popular music is largely rhythmical. The same appeal of pulse is predominant in all other arts which are oral. The pulse of poetry must be regular; the performance of a prose drama must be well-timed or pulsed. In all things the human brain demands symmetry and proportion so as to give unity and understanding to what is going on. An auditor will subconsciously arrange reiterated sound into regular periods of stress and relaxation.[1]

[1] See page 11: "Rhythm and Harmony in Music and Poetry."—Raymond.

Pulse is apparent in all things. Our breathing, method of walking, heartbeat, and daily life. In nature, the seasons, the tide, the flying of a bird and most bird-calls.

The majority of books upon the theory of music deal with sound and form, but say little or nothing about rhythm. There seems to be no definite meaning or consistency in the terminology used. It is difficult to understand why this vital factor in musical composition and interpretation has been neglected. The result is that here in America, the home of syncopation, the music pupil displays little real rhythmic sense in his performance. That this defect has been universal may be gathered from the following quotation in the "Philosophy of Music" by William Pole (1877): "Although the feeling for regular periodical movement is undoubtedly a natural one, yet experience in practical music shows that it is far from being universal. Every music teacher knows to his cost, that to get the time of music properly attended to is usually the most difficult and uphill part of his task."

TERMINOLOGY

Poetry and music were inseparable in the beginning. The music followed the metrical and rhythmical division and the inflection of the poetry. It is logical, that as music became independent of poetry, it must have preserved the fundamental principles of poetic meter and rhythm.

Meter in poetry is the feeling of pulse which is set up by the regular recurrence of stressed syllables. Meter is determined by the number of stressed syllables in a line. The line is made apparent to the auditor by a pause or rhyme. There may be from two to seven or eight stressed syllables in a line. A line with two stressed syllables is in dimeter; with three stressed syllables, in trimeter; four, in tetrameter; five, in pentameter; six in hexameter; seven, in heptameter.

Rhythm in poetry is the grouping of stressed and relaxed, or long and short syllables, into feet. The common poetic feet in English are:

| Iambus ∪ — | Trochee — ∪ | Spondee — — |
| Anapest ∪ ∪ — | Dactyl — ∪ ∪ | Amphibrach ∪ — ∪ |

The number of relaxed syllables may vary throughout a poem, but the stressed syllables will recur at regular intervals. The rhythm of a poem is determined by the predominating foot. In the following lines of Longfellow the meter is tetrameter (four feet to a line) the rhythm iambic:

And then | the blue | eyed Norse | man told |
 ∪   —   ∪   —   ∪   —   ∪   —
A Sa | ga of | the days | of old. |
 ∪ —   ∪ —   ∪   —   ∪ —

Meter or *Time* in music is the feeling of pulse which is set up by the regular recurrence of stress. Meter is determined by the number of stressed pulses in a musical phrase. The phrase is made apparent to the auditor by a pause called a cadence.

There is duple meter, a stressed pulse followed by a relaxed pulse:

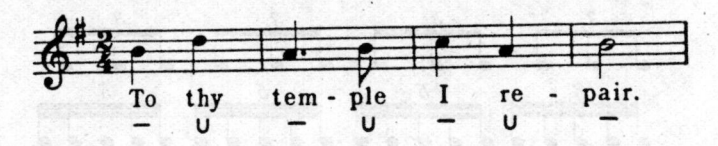

To thy tem - ple I re - pair.
 — ∪   —   ∪ — ∪ —

Triple meter, a stressed pulse followed by two relaxed pulses:

Sun of my soul, thou Sav - iour dear
 — ∪ ∪   —   [∪] ∪ — [∪] ∪ —[∪ ∪]

[1] The bar used in scansion marks off the poetic foot. It is not necessarily drawn before the long or stressed syllables as in music. In this example the musical bar would come before "then," "blue," etc.

Quadruple meter, a stressed pulse followed by three relaxed pulses:

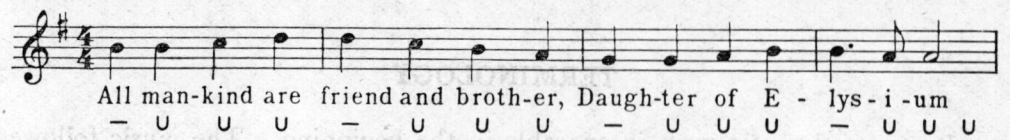

All man-kind are friend and broth-er, Daugh-ter of E - lys-i-um
 — ᴗ ᴗ   —   ᴗ ᴗ   —   ᴗ ᴗ   —   ᴗ ᴗ

Rhythm in music is the arrangement of notes differing in mathematical value upon the pulses of the meter, a definite note-value having been assigned to the metric pulse. The following note-values and their equivalent rests are used in music: the breve ‖𝅜‖ or rest 𝄺 , the whole note 𝅝 or rest 𝄻 , the half-note 𝅗𝅥 or rest 𝄼 , the quarter-note 𝅘𝅥 or rest 𝄽 , the eighth-note 𝅘𝅥𝅮 or rest 𝄾 , the sixteenth-note 𝅘𝅥𝅯 or rest 𝄿 , the thirty-second note 𝅘𝅥𝅰 or rest 𝅀 , the sixty-fourth-note 𝅘𝅥𝅱 or rest 𝅁 , the one-hundred and twenty-eighth-note 𝅘𝅥𝅲 or rest 𝅂 .

The whole, half-, quarter-, eighth-, and the sixteenth-note may be used as rhythmic units, the quarter-note being the most common.

Rhythmic subdivisions are made by dividing the pulse by two or the multiple of two. The following subdivisions are found in duple, triple, and quadruple meters, using the quarter-note as the rhythmic unit:

The following terms are commonly used:

Rhythmic unit. The kind of note ascribed to the metric pulse. In 2/4 the quarter-note, in 2/2 the half-note.

Rhythmic figure. The grouping of notes of different value into a pattern which is reproduced throughout the composition.

2/4 𝄾 𝅘𝅥𝅯𝅘𝅥𝅯𝅘𝅥𝅯 𝅗𝅥 | Beethoven, 5th Symphony   2/4 𝅘𝅥𝅮𝅘𝅥𝅯𝅘𝅥𝅯 𝅘𝅥 𝅘𝅥 | Beethoven, 7th Symphony

Uniform rhythm. When notes of the same value are employed throughout a phrase.

Doxology

Regular rhythm. When the longer notes occupy the accented pulse of the meter.

Blue Bells of Scotland

Irregular rhythm. When the shorter notes occupy the accented pulse of the meter.

Haydn

Syncopated rhythm. When the longer notes occupy the unaccented fractions of the pulses.

Beethoven

Measure. The grouping of the stressed and relaxed pulses forming the meter.

Bar. A vertical line drawn across the staff to show the stressed pulse of the measure.

In duple meter the pulses may be arranged in a measure either

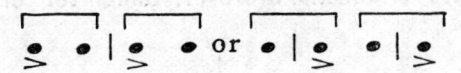

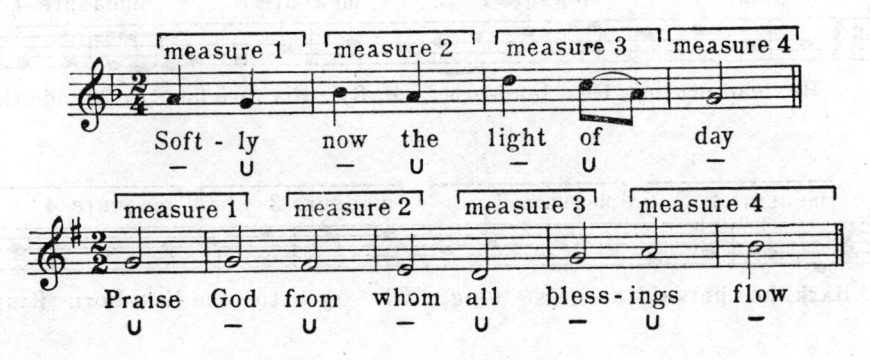

Soft - ly now the light of day

Praise God from whom all bless-ings flow

In triple meter the pulses may be arranged

a   b   c

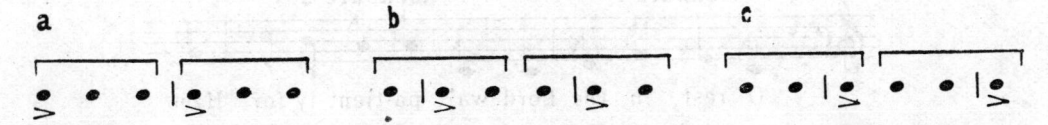

In quadruple meter the pulses may be arranged

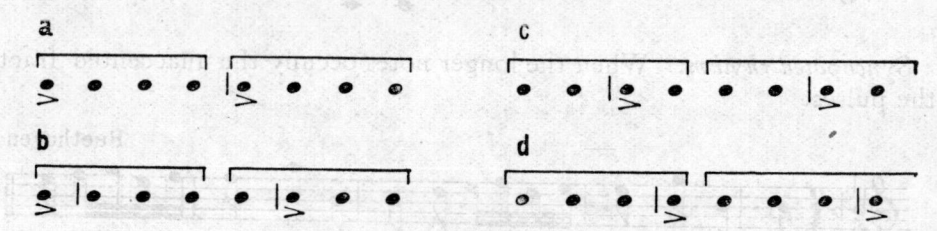

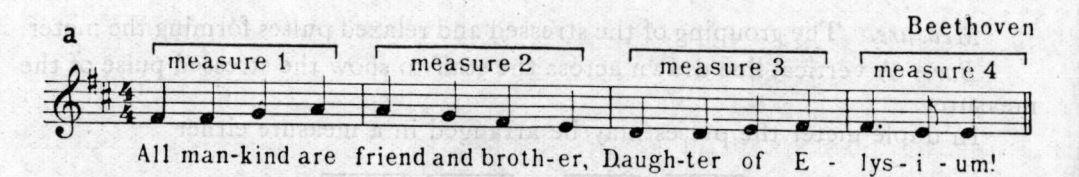

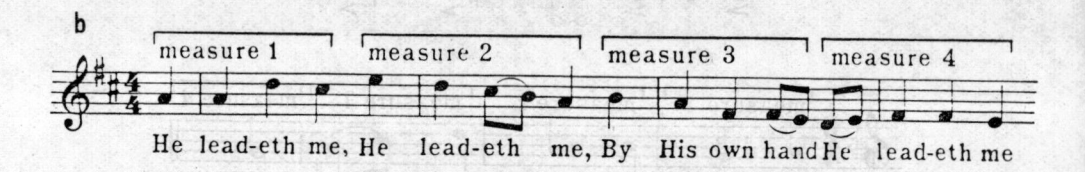

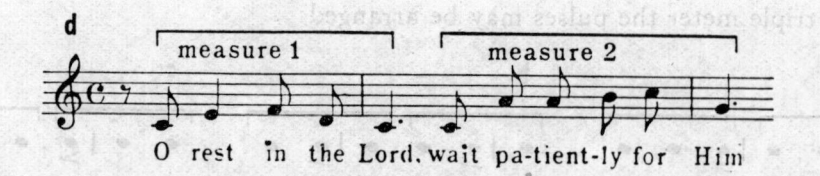

The meter and the rhythmic unit are designated by two numbers placed one above the other at the beginning of a composition; the upper number giving the meter, the lower number the rhythmic unit. This is commonly called the *Time Signature*.

2 = Duple Meter
4 = A quarter-note or its equivalent to a pulse

2 = Duple Meter
2 = A half-note or its equivalent to a pulse

It has been found by experiment that it is most natural to divide pulses into twos and fours; but at certain speeds there is a tendency to subdivide into three and six.[1] In reading poetry it is quite natural to read the foot — ᴗ as — Ⓤ ᴗ (Mary / Mary). This is possibly due to the fact that in the scansion of classical languages, long syllables were given twice the length of time as the others. When this triplet subdivision occurs in music, we have what is generally called the *Compound Meters:*

The six-pulse meter, which is a compound of duple meter

The nine-pulse meter, which is a compound of triple meter

The twelve-pulse meter, which is a compound of quadruple meter.

[1] See page 11: "Rhythm and Harmony in Music and Poetry."—Raymond.

The eighth-note is most used as a rhythmic unit in compound meters. The rhythms resulting from the triplet subdivisions are:

These rhythmic effects could be expressed in the simple meters, but the irregular rhythmic subdivision would necessitate the writing of a numeral over each irregular group.

A five-pulse meter is a combination of a duple and triple measure. The grouping is designated either by phrase-marks or beaming as in Tschaikowsky, or by dotted bars as in the Vidal example.

Tschaikowsky, 6th Symphony

Vidal, Ariette

A seven-pulse meter is a combination of a triple and quadruple measure:

Saint-Saëns, "La Solitaire"

Two time-signatures are frequently used by modern composers: Goldmark in "Sakuntala" uses $\frac{3}{4}\frac{9}{8}$, meaning that at any time he may use the rhythmic figures formed by subdividing into two or three.

In vocal music the voice-part is often in a different meter from the accompaniment. The voice part of Dvořák's "Als die alte Mutter" is in 2/4, the accompaniment is in 6/8.

When there are rhythmic subdivisions in instrumental music, the metric pulses are made apparent to the eye by joining the stems of the notes with a straight line called a *beam*.

In present-day notation, beams are not carried over the bar except in the rare cases when they are used to show a rhythmic figure.

Wüllner

In quadruple meter, when the rhythmic subdivision is into two, the first two or the last two pulses may be beamed together, but never the second and the third pulses.

Smaller subdivisions should be beamed separately for each pulse.

When thirty-second and sixty-fourth-notes are used, the beaming is arranged so that the eye will grasp the subdivision of the pulse.

Haydn

In vocal music each word and syllable is given a separate note. Beaming is employed only when several notes are sung to one vowel sound.

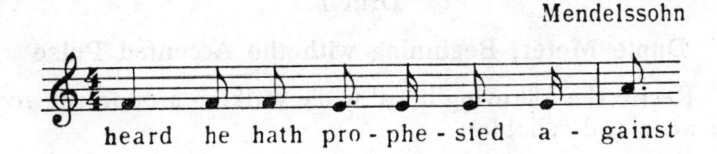

Mendelssohn

heard   he   hath   pro - phe - sied   a - gainst

PUPILS AND RHYTHM

With the natural feeling for pulse and the simple mathematical rhythmic subdivisions, it seems strange that this universal difficulty with time in music should exist. A pupil will perform drills in rhythm perfectly, yet there will be no apparent application of the rhythmic sense in his playing. This may be due to several reasons; carelessness on the part of teacher and pupil, lack of definite knowledge on the subject, lack of technical facility, and the following physical fact.

The meter is natural, therefore physical, and is expressed by physical motion. One cannot hear music with a marked pulse without responding to it with the movement of the head, foot, or arm. When a band plays a march, one steps in time with the pulse and not the many tones played. One who dances to the exhilarating syncopation of modern jazz, steps with the pulse, not the syncopation. The rhythmic subdivisions and figures are man-made, the result of artistic creation and therefore mental. The physical expression of pulse enables one to maintain balance. The ability to form rhythms is entirely a question of mental conception and development. The physical expression of rhythms upsets the balance of the phrase and generally makes analysis impossible. Imagine the results with an orchestra playing the "Star-Spangled Banner" if the conductor gave a beat for each note instead of for each pulse. In analyzing rhythms, thought or heard, one instinctively keeps time with finger or foot and analyzes the number and arrangement of notes upon each pulse. In playing the piano it is not possible to give physical expression of the pulse The performance of rhythms requires physical exertion, therefore the balance of the pulse is lost. There are many evidences of this desire to express pulse physically. A so-called jazz player brings the foot down upon the loud pedal with each pulse. He will move his arms and sometimes the entire upper part of his body in time with the pulse. If he "fakes" the bass, the physical movement of the left hand keeps time. The performer upon the violin, flute, etc., and the singer keep time with their feet. Even some of the great orchestral conductors keep time with their feet in moments of great excitement. Unless a pianist, and, to a lesser degree, other performers are properly trained, or strongly endowed with a feeling of pulse, the physical execution of rhythms will tend to upset their balance.

From the rhythmic standpoint of interpretation, there is much more involved than the mere keeping of pulse and the correct rendition of rhythmic figures. (This will be treated in later chapters.) The pupil must first master the mechanical keeping of time and the playing of rhythms before he can hope to approach the more subtle aspects of interpretation.

DRILLS FOR THE STUDY OF METER

Drill I

Duple Meter, Beginning with the Accented Pulse

1. (a) Recite the following lines[1] while walking around the room, taking a step for each word and syllable:

[1]In all of the following exercises where the instructions are for the pianist to play, the violin student should use the violin and the vocal student should sing, keeping time with the arm movement.

Jack and Jill went up the hill.
Simple Simon met a pieman.
Noah of old did build an ark.
Mary had a little lamb.
Tell me where is fancy bred?
Water, water, everywhere.

(b) Recite the lines, repeating each several times. Beat down and up, allowing the arm to fall at each stressed syllable. Arm movement: ↓↑

(c) Copy each line and draw a bar before each stressed syllable.
Jack and | Jill went | up the | hill.

(d) Transcribe each line into note-values in 2/2, 2/4 and 2/8.

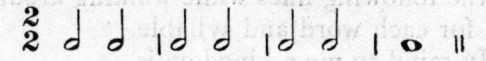

(e) Beating down and up, sing the words on the pitches 1, 3, 5, 8, 5, 3, 1.

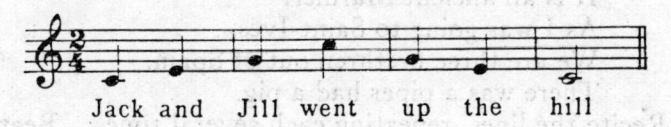

Jack and   Jill went   up   the   hill

(f) Reciting slowly a word for each note, play the following exercises first with the right hand, then with the left hand, then with both hands:

2. Play the following melodies, keeping strict time and counting aloud "one, two"—"one, two":

3. Play the following piano composition, counting aloud:

Andante

Drill II

Duple Meter, Beginning with the Unaccented Pulse

1. (a) Recite the following lines while walking around the room, taking a step for each word and syllable.
    My mind to me a kingdom is.
    A man's a man for all o' that.
    It is an ancient Mariner.
    As I was going to Saint-Ives.
    We are three brethren out of Spain.
    There was a piper had a pig.
   (b) Recite the lines, repeating each several times. Beat up and down allowing the arm to fall at each stressed syllable. Arm movement: ↑↓
   (c) Copy each line and draw a bar before each stressed syllable.
   (d) Transcribe each line into note-values in 2/2, 2/4 and 2/8.
   (e) Beating up and down, sing the words on the pitches 1, 3, 5, 8.

   The shades of night were fall-ing fast

   (f) Reciting slowly a word or syllable for each note, play the following exercises first with the right hand, then with the left hand, and then with both hands:

2. Play the following melodies, keeping strict time and counting aloud "two, one"—"two, one." Note that in melodies 5 and 6, though the notes between the bars are beamed together, they are not related. The note before the bar belongs to the note following, as each measure begins with the up-beat.

3. Play the following piano composition, counting aloud:

Maestoso

Drill III

Triple Meter, Beginning with the Accented Pulse

1. (a) Recite the following lines while walking around the room, taking a step for each word and syllable:

> Onward the bridal procession now moved.
> "Forward the light brigade, charge for the guns," he said.
> Grimly with swords that were sharp from the stone.
> Hey diddle diddle, the cat and the fiddle.

(b) Recite the lines, repeating each line several times, beating down, out and up.

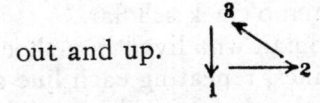

(c) Copy each line and draw a bar before each stressed syllable.
(d) Transcribe each line into note-values in 3/2, 3/4 and 3/8.
(e) Beating time, sing the words to the following pitches:

(f) Reciting slowly a word or syllable for each note, play the following exercises first with the right hand, then with the left hand, then with both hands:

2. Play the following melodies, keeping strict time and counting aloud "one, two, three"—"one, two, three."

3. Play the following piano composition, counting aloud:
Moderato

Drill IV
Triple Meter, Beginning with the Third Pulse

1. (a) Recite the following lines while walking around the room, taking a step for each word and syllable:

>Most friendship is feigning, most loving mere folly.
>A corpulent man is my bachelor chum.
>To market, to market, a gallop, a trot.
>A diller, a dollar, a ten o'clock scholar.
>There was an old woman who lived in a shoe.

(b) Beating time, recite the lines, repeating each line several times.
(c) Copy each line and draw a bar before each stressed syllable.
(d) Transcribe each line in note-values in 3/2, 3/4 and 3/8.
(e) Beating time, sing the words to the following pitches:

(f) Reciting a word or syllable for each note, play the following exercises first with the right hand, then with the left hand, then with both hands:

To indicate the phrasing, it is necessary to lift the hand after the 3d note, thus shortening its value by a very small fraction.

2. Play the following melodies, keeping strict time and counting aloud:

3. Play the following piano composition, counting aloud:

Religioso

Drill V

Triple Meter Beginning with the Second Pulse

1. (a) Recite the following lines while walking around the room, taking a step for each word and syllable:

> 'Tis the middle of night by the old castle clock.
> 'Twas the night before Christmas and all through the house,
> Not a creature was stirring, not even a mouse.
> When a twister a-twisting will twist him a twist.

(b) Beating time, recite the lines, repeating each several times.
(c) Copy each line and draw a bar before each stressed syllable.
(d) Transcribe each line in note-values in 3/2, 3/4 and 3/8.
(e) Beating time, sing the words to the following pitches:

(f) Reciting a word or syllable for each note, play the following exercises first with the right hand, then with the left hand, then with both hands:

In beginning on the second beat, it is necessary to feel and express the stress of the first pulse by some physical movement; either a backward movement of the head or the lifting of the hand. The first two notes should be played and sung without weight and in a curve leading up to the weight or stress on the pulse after the bar.

2. Play the following melodies, keeping strict time and counting aloud:

3. Play the following piano composition counting aloud:
Moderato

Drill VI
Quadruple Meter, Beginning with the Accented Pulse

1. (a) Recite the following lines while walking around the room, taking a step for each word and syllable:

Love took up the harp of life and smote on all the chords with might.
Listen to the Indian Legend, to the song of Hiawatha!
Tom he was a piper's son, he learned to play when he was young.
Little Tommy Tittlemouse, lived in a little house.

(b) Beating time, recite the lines, repeating each line several times.

Arm movement:

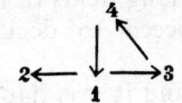

(c) Copy each line and draw a bar before each stressed syllable.
(d) Transcribe each line into note-values in 4/2, 4/4 and 4/8.
(e) Beating time, sing the words to the following pitches:

(f) Reciting a word or syllable for each note, play the following exercises first with the right hand, then with the left hand, then with both hands:

2. Play the following melodies, keeping strict time and counting aloud:

3. Play the following piano composition, counting aloud:

Andante espressivo

p

Drill VII
Quadruple Meter, Beginning with the Fourth Pulse

1. (a) Recite the following lines while walking around the room, taking a step with each word and syllable:

   The poet in a golden clime was born, with golden stars above.
   On either side the river lie long fields of barley and of rye.
   Forthwith the crowd proceed to deck with halter'd noose M'Fingal's neck.
   I had a little hobby-horse and it was dapple gray.
   There was a crooked woman and she went a crooked mile.

   (b) Beating time, recite the lines, repeating each line several times.
   (c) Copy each line and draw a bar before each stressed syllable.
   (d) Transcribe each line into note-values in 4/2, 4/4 and 4/8.
   (e) Beating time, sing the words to the following pitches:

   (f) Reciting a word or syllable for each note, play the following exercises first with the right hand, then with the left hand, then with both hands:

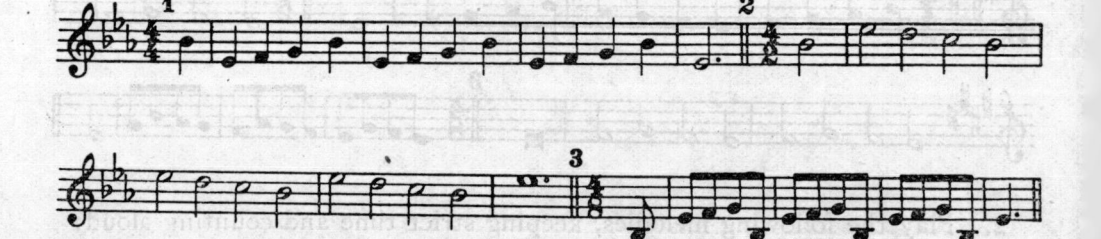

2. Play the following melodies, keeping strict time and counting aloud:

3. Play the following piano composition, counting aloud:

Andante

Drill VIII
Quadruple Meter, Beginning with the Third Pulse

1. (a) Recite the following lines while walking around the room, keeping step with each word and syllable:

> For I dipped into the future far as human eye could see.
> And the happy stars above them seemed to brighten as they passed.
> From the hollow reeds he fashioned flutes so musical and mellow.
> Sneeze on Monday, sneeze for danger; sneeze on Tuesday, kiss a stranger.

(b) Beating time, recite the lines, repeating each line several times.
(c) Copy each line and draw a bar before each stressed syllable.
(d) Transcribe each line into note-values in 4/2, 4/4 and 4/8.
(e) Beating time, sing the words to the following pitches:

(f) Reciting a word or syllable for each note, play the following exercises first with the right hand, then with the left hand, then with both hands:

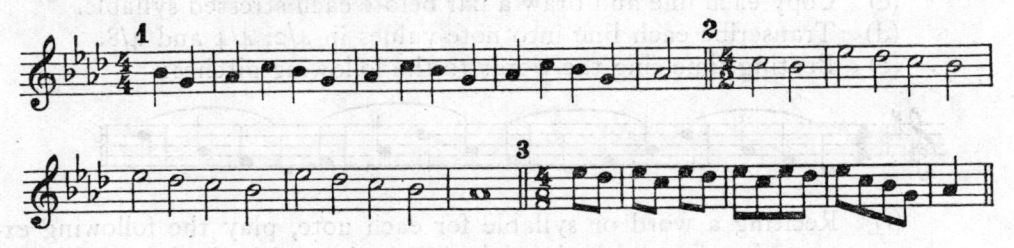

2. Play the following melodies, keeping strict time and counting aloud:

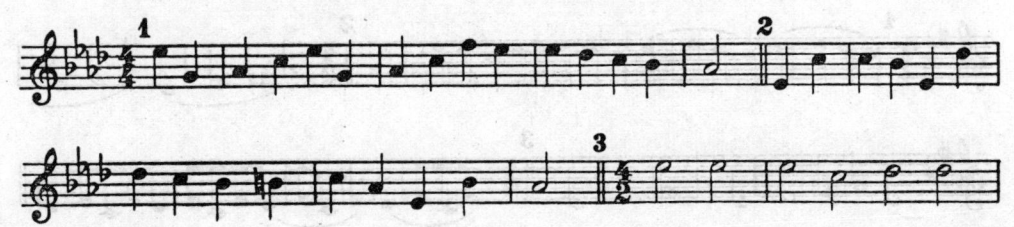

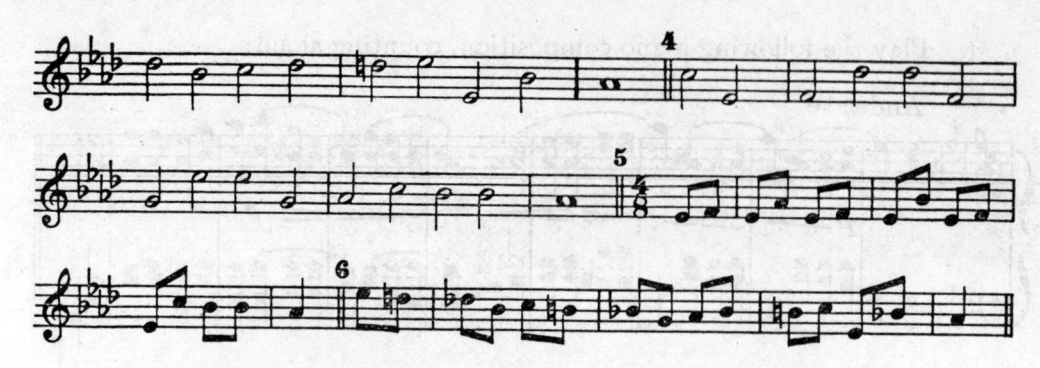

3. Play the following piano composition, counting aloud:

Tempo di Gavotta

Drill IX

Quadruple Meter, Beginning with the Second Pulse

1. (a) Recite the following lines while walking around the room, keeping step with each word and syllable:

> When I am living in the midlands that are sodden and unkind.
> Just now the lilac is in bloom and all before my little room.
> I charge my daughters, everyone, to keep good house while I am gone.
> We are three brethren out of Spain who come to court your daughter Jane.

(b) Beating time, recite the lines, repeating each line several times.
(c) Copy each line and draw a bar before each stressed syllable.
(d) Transcribe each line into note-values in 4/2, 4/4 and 4/8.
(e) Beating time sing the words to the following pitches:

(f) Reciting a word or syllable for each note, play the following exercises first with the right hand, then with the left, then with both hands:

RHYTHM IN MUSIC

2. Play the following melodies, keeping strict time and counting aloud:

3. Play the following piano composition, counting aloud:

Andante

DRILLS FOR THE STUDY OF RHYTHM

Drill X

In the preceding exercises the rhythm has been uniform, a note for each metric pulse, except in the last measure. Rhythms are formed by the addition or the subdivision of the rhythmic unit ascribed to the pulse of the meter.

Added Pulses and Rests in Duple Meter

1. (a) Recite the poetic lines given in Drill 1, page 11, while walking around the room, taking a step for each word and syllable.
 (b) Continue walking at the same pace, recite the lines omitting every other word, ex. Jack — Jill — up — hill —.
 (c) Transcribe each spoken word and syllable into note-values, and each omitted word into rest-values in 2/2, 2/4, 2/8.

 (d) Repeat as in (b), sustaining the spoken word or syllable during the time occupied by the omitted words or syllables.

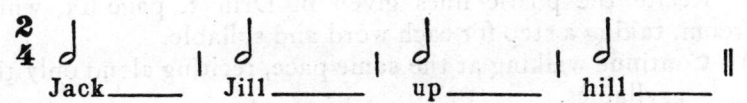

(e) Transcribe each word or syllable into note-values in 2/2, 2/4, 2/8.
(f) Repeat the same practice, using the arm movement for duple meter, and sing each line on the following pitches:

(g) Repeat the exercise omitting every other word or syllable, and sing as in 1, then sustaining the first word as in 2.

(h) Reciting slowly, play the following exercises first with the right hand, then with the left hand, then with both hands:

2. Play the following melodies, keeping strict time and counting aloud:

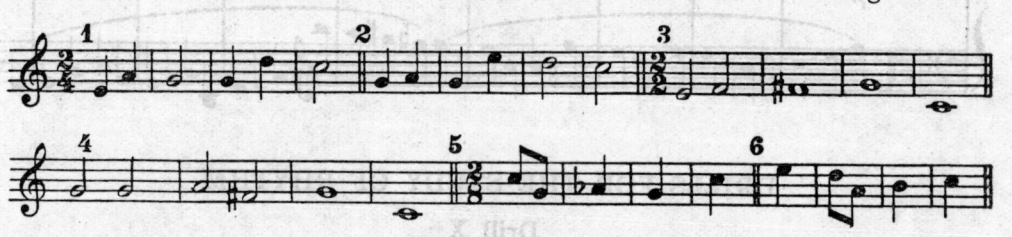

3. Play the following piano composition, counting aloud:

Andante

Drill XI

Added Pulses in Triple Meter

(The $\bm{\dotted{\quarter}}$.)

1. (a) Recite the poetic lines given in Drill 3, page 13, while walking around the room, taking a step for each word and syllable.
 (b) Continue walking at the same pace, reciting aloud only the stressed syllables.

(c) Transcribe each syllable into note- and rest-values in 3/2, 3/4, 3/8.

Grim - - swords - - sharp - - stone - -

(d) Repeat as in (b), sustaining the spoken word or syllable during the time occupied by the omitted word or syllables.

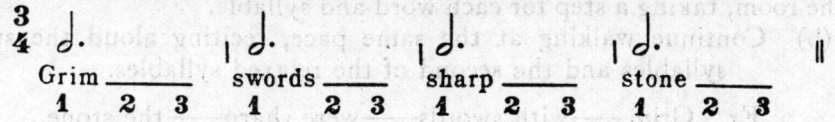

Grim ____ swords ____ sharp ____ stone ____
1 2 3   1 2 3   1 2 3   1 2 3

(e) Transcribe each syllable into note-values in 3/2, 3/4 and 3/8.
(f) Repeat the same practice, using the arm movement for triple meter, and sing each line on the following pitches:

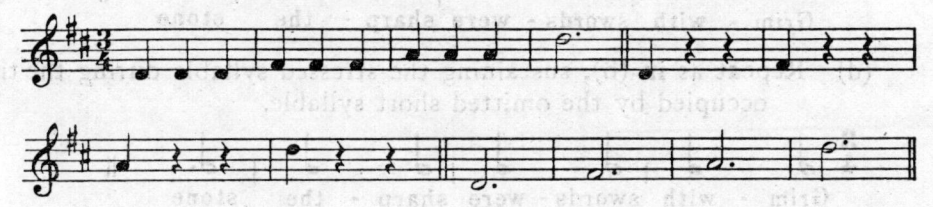

(g) Reciting slowly, play the following exercises first with the right hand, then with the left hand, then with both hands:

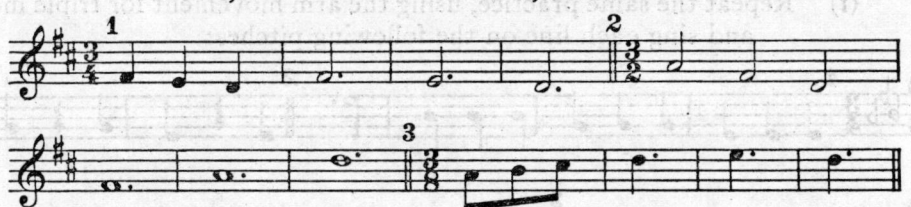

2. Play the following melodies, keeping strict time and counting aloud:

3. Play the following piano composition, counting aloud:

Weber

Drill XII
Added Pulses in Triple Meter

(The ♩ ♩. = 3/4)

1. (a) Recite the poetic lines given in Drill 3, page 13, while walking around the room, taking a step for each word and syllable.

    (b) Continue walking at the same pace, reciting aloud the stressed syllables and the second of the relaxed syllables.

    Ex.: Grim——with swords——were sharp——the stone.

    (c) Transcribe each syllable into note- and rest-values in 3/2, 3/4, 3/8.

    Grim - with swords - were sharp - the stone

    (d) Repeat as in (b), sustaining the stressed syllable during the time occupied by the omitted short syllable.

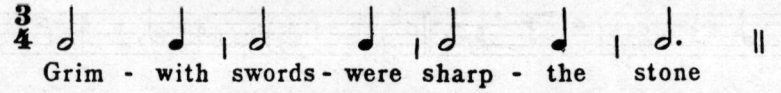

    Grim - with swords - were sharp - the stone

    (e) Transcribe each syllable into note-values of 3/2, 3/4, 3/8.

    (f) Repeat the same practice, using the arm movement for triple meter, and sing each line on the following pitches:

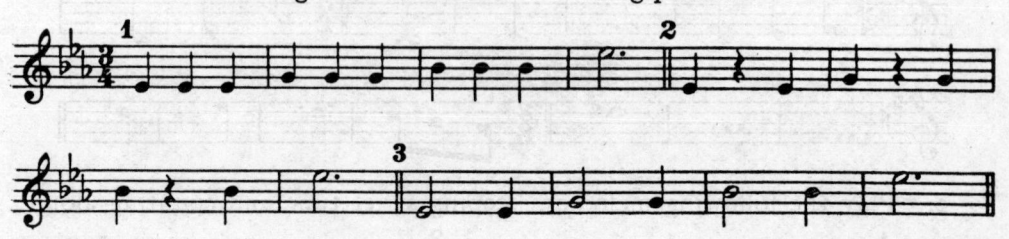

    (g) Reciting slowly, play the following exercises, first with the right hand, then with the left hand, then with both hands:

2. Play the following melodies, keeping strict time and counting aloud:

3. Play the following piano composition, counting aloud:

Adagio

Drill XIII
The Quadruple Meter

(The ♩)

1. (a) Recite the poetic lines given in Drill 6, page 17, while walking around the room, taking a step for each word and syllable.
   (b) Continue walking at the same pace, reciting aloud the stressed syllables.

Tom - - - pip - - - learned - - - he

   (c) Transcribe into note- and rest-values in 4/2, 4/4, 4/8.
   (d) Continue walking, reciting aloud the stressed syllables and the second of the relaxed syllables.

Tom - was - pip - son - learned - play - he - young

   (e) Transcribe each syllable into note- and rest-values in 4/2, 4/4 and 4/8.
   (f) Repeat as in (b) and (d), sustaining the spoken syllable during the time occupied by the omitted syllable.

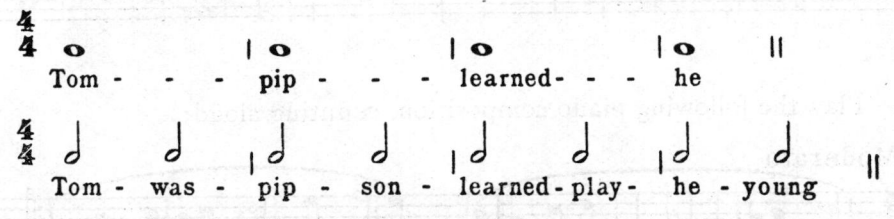

Tom - - - pip - - - learned - - - he

Tom - was - pip - son - learned - play - he - young

   (g) Transcribe each syllable into note-values in 4/2, 4/4 and 4/8.
   (h) Beating time, sing each line on the following pitches:

(g) Reciting slowly, play the following exercises first with the right hand, then with the left hand, then with both hands:

2. Play the following melodies, keeping strict time and counting aloud:

3. Play the following piano composition, counting aloud:

Moderato

Drill XIV
The Quadruple Meter

(The ♩.)

1. (a) Recite the poetic lines given in Drill 7, page 18, while walking around the room, taking a step with each word and syllable.
   (b) Continue walking at the same pace, reciting aloud the stressed syllables and the preceding relaxed syllables.

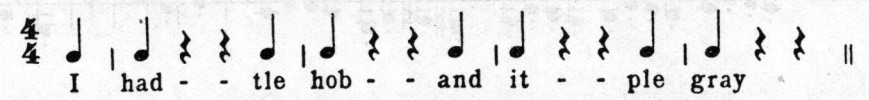

I had - - tle hob - - and it - - ple gray

   (c) Transcribe each syllable into note- and rest-values in 4/2, 4/4, 4/8.
   (d) Repeat as in (b) sustaining the stressed syllable during the time occupied by the omitted syllables.

I had - - tle hob - - and it - - ple gray

   (e) Transcribe each syllable into note-values in 4/2, 4/4, 4/8.
   (f) Beating time sing each line on the following pitches:

   (g) Reciting slowly, play the following exercises first with the right hand, then with the left hand, then with both hands:

2. Play the following melodies, keeping strict time and counting aloud:

3. Play the following piano composition counting aloud:

Pomposo

THE SUBDIVISION OF PULSES

Drill XV

The Subdivision into Two

1. (a) March at a moderate tempo, feeling the left foot to be the stressed pulse, the right the relaxed pulse in duple meter. Visualize this in note-values in 2/4 as you march.

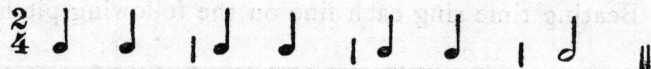

   (b) Continue marching and recite the following two syllable words with each step:
   Walking, marching, singing, playing, dancing.

   (c) Repeat visualization of the notations in 2/4.

2. (a) Repeat the following lines, using the arm movement for duple meter and reciting a poetic foot to each pulse:
   Sweetly singing, sweetly singing, sweetly singing songs.
   Spritely dancing, spritely dancing, spritely dancing fauns.
   Swiftly flying, swiftly flying, swiftly flying birds.

   (b) Copy each line and transcribe into note-values in 2/2, 2/4 and 2/8.

   (c) Reciting the lines in the same tempo, play the following exercises first with the right hand, then with the left hand, then with both hands:

3. Play the following melodies keeping strict time and counting aloud:

RHYTHM IN MUSIC

4. Play the following piano compositions, counting aloud:

Allegro

p leggero

Andante

p

Adagio

Drill XVI
The Subdivision into Four

1. (a) Recite the following four-syllable words while walking about the room:

   Difficulty, interesting, circumstances, Hiawatha, delicately.

   (b) Repeat visualization of the notations in 2/4.

2. (a) Repeat the following line, using the arm movement for duple meter reciting a word to each pulse:

   Improvising, improvising, improvising, improvising, improvising, improvising songs.

   January, February, January, February, January, February, March.

   (b) Copy the line and transcribe into note-values in 2/2, 2/4 and 2/8.
   (c) Reciting the line in the same tempo, play the following exercises first with the right hand, then with the left hand, then with both hands:

3. Play the following melodies, keeping strict time and counting aloud:

4. Play the following piano compositions, counting aloud:

Beethoven

Drill XVII

The Subdivision into Three

1. (a) Recite the following three-syllable words while walking about the room:

    Lubricate, tenement, elegance, institute, musical.

    (b) Repeat visualization of the notations in 2/4 and 6/8.

2. (a) Repeat the following lines, using the arm movement for duple meter, reciting a word to each pulse:

    Merrily, merrily, merrily, merrily, merrily, merrily sing.
    Practising, practising, practising, practising, practising, practising, Bach.

    (b) Copy each line and transcribe into note-values in 2/4 and 6/8.
    (c) Reciting the line in the same tempo, play the following exercises first with the right hand, then with the left hand, then with both hands:

3. Play the following melodies, keeping strict time and counting aloud:

4. Play the following piano compositions, counting aloud:

Beethoven

p sempre dolce

34 RHYTHM IN MUSIC

Allegro   Beethoven

Clementi

Drill XVIII

The Addition of Pulses in 6/8 Time

(The 𝅘𝅥𝅭 and 𝅘𝅥 𝅘𝅥𝅮)

1. Play the following exercises, counting aloud, first with the right hand, then with the left hand, then with both hands:

RHYTHM IN MUSIC

2. Play the following melodies, keeping strict time and counting aloud:

3. Play the following piano composition, counting aloud:

Andante

Drill XIX

The 𝅗𝅥. and 𝅗𝅥 𝅘𝅥𝅮 in 9/8 Time

1. Play the following exercises, counting aloud, first with the right hand, then with the left hand, then with both hands:

2. Play the following melodies, keeping strict time and counting aloud:

3. Play the following piano composition, counting aloud, first with the right hand, then with the left hand, then with both hands:

Andante espressivo

Drill XX

The ♩. and ♩ ♪ in 12/8 Time

1. Play the following exercises, counting aloud:

2. Play the following melodies, keeping strict time and counting aloud:

3. Play the following piano composition, counting aloud:

Adagio
pp

Drill XXI

The Subdivision into Six

1. Play the following exercise, counting aloud, first with the right hand, then with the left hand, then with both hands:

RHYTHM IN MUSIC

2. Play the following melodies, keeping strict time and counting aloud:

3. Play the following piano composition, counting aloud:

Allegro

Drill XXII

The ♩ ♫ in 6/8 Time

1. Play the following exercises, counting aloud, first with the right hand, then with the left hand, then with both hands:

2. Play the following melodies, keeping strict time and counting aloud:

3. Play the following piano composition, counting aloud:

Allegretto

Drill XXIII

The ♫ in Duple Meter

1. Play the following exercise, counting aloud, first with the right hand, then with the left hand, then with both hands:

2. Play the following melodies, keeping strict time and counting aloud:

3. Play the following piano composition, counting aloud:

Vivace

THE COMBINATION OF ADDED AND DIVIDED PULSES

Drill XXIV

Two- Three- and Four-Pulse Meter

The recitation of a stanza of any nursery rhyme will disclose the fact that while the stressed syllables fall at regular intervals, the relaxed syllables are very irregular, sometimes one and again two and at times both the stressed and relaxed syllables are omitted. For example:

Mary, Mary, quite contrary
− ᴗ − ᴗ −   ᴗ − ᴗ

How does your garden grow
− ᴗ ᴗ − ᴗ − [ᴗ −]

With cockle shells and silver bells
ᴗ − ᴗ −   ᴗ − ᴗ −

And pretty maids all in a row.
ᴗ − ᴗ ᴗ − ᴗ ᴗ − [ᴗ − ᴗ]

     − ᴗ |−   ᴗ |−   ᴗ |− ᴗ

     − ᴗ ᴗ |−   ᴗ |− [ᴗ |−]

     − ᴗ − ᴗ |− ᴗ |− ᴗ |−

     ᴗ − ᴗ ᴗ |− ᴗ ᴗ |− [ᴗ |−]

The short syllable at the beginning of lines 3 and 4 belongs to the preceding foot.

Hark, hark,
[ᴗ] − [ᴗ] −

The dogs do bark
ᴗ − ᴗ −

The beggars are coming to town
ᴗ − ᴗ ᴗ − ᴗ ᴗ − [ᴗ −]

Some in rags
[ᴗ] − ᴗ −

Some in tags
[ᴗ] − ᴗ −

Some in velvet gowns.
[ᴗ] − ᴗ − ᴗ − [ᴗ −]

     [ᴗ] − |[ᴗ] − |

     ᴗ − |ᴗ − |

     ᴗ − |ᴗ ᴗ − |ᴗ − [ᴗ −]

     [ᴗ] − |ᴗ − |

     [ᴗ] − |ᴗ − |

     [ᴗ] − |ᴗ − |ᴗ − [ᴗ −]

These stanzas would be expressed in musical notation as follows:

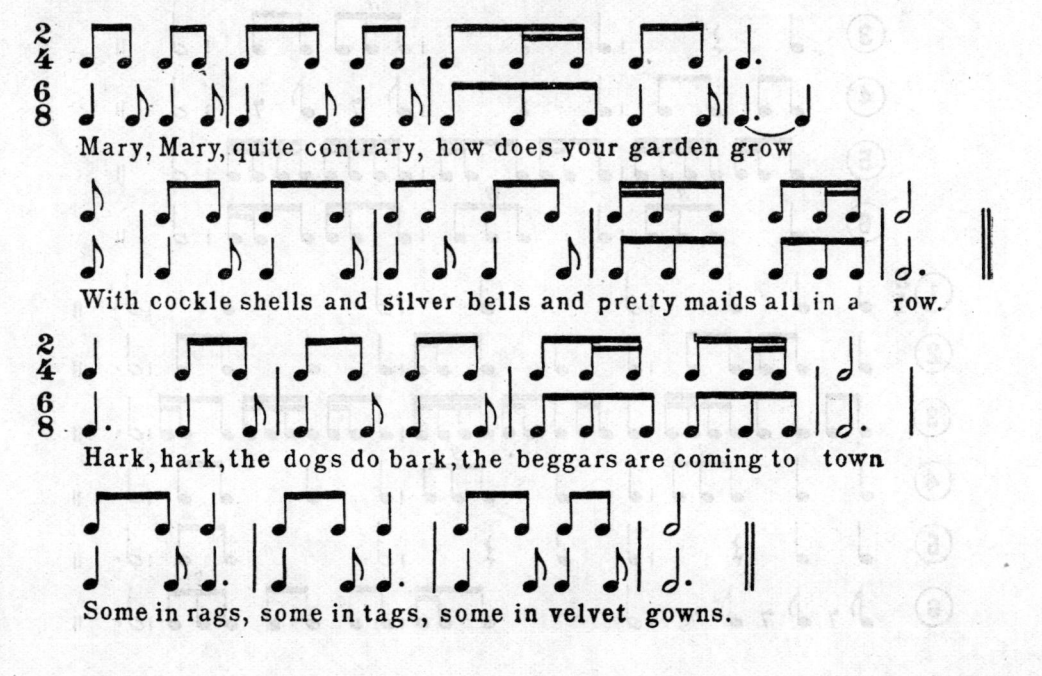

Mary, Mary, quite contrary, how does your garden grow

With cockle shells and silver bells and pretty maids all in a row.

Hark, hark, the dogs do bark, the beggars are coming to town

Some in rags, some in tags, some in velvet gowns.

1. (a) Recite and make poetic scansions of the following nursery rhymes.

   Jack and Jill went up the hill
   To fetch a pail of water;
   Jack fell down and broke his crown
   And Jill came tumbling after.

   Little Miss Muffet
   Sat on a tuffet,
   Eating her curds and whey;
   Along came a spider,
   And sat down beside her,
   And frightened Miss Muffet away.

   Baa, baa, black sheep, have you any wool?
   Yes sir, yes sir, three bags full;
   One for the master, and one for my dame,
   One for the little boy who lives down the lane.

   A hundred years is a very long time,
   Yo, heave, ho!
   And yet 'tis said they were singing this rime
   A hundred years ago.

   (b) Make rhythmic outlines for the above poems.
   (c) Practice the following exercises, beating time and singing on a major scale. For example, No. 1:

RHYTHM IN MUSIC

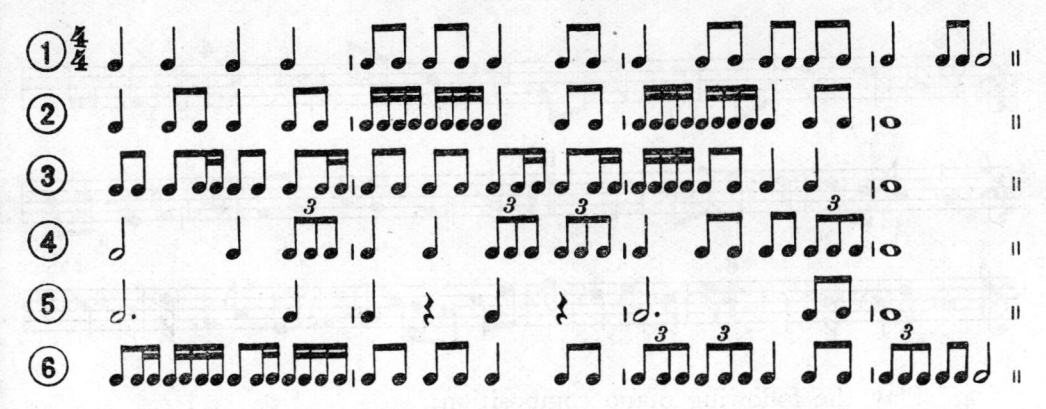

[Rhythm exercises 1–6 in 4/4 time]

(d) Play the above exercises in a major scale, first with the right hand, then with the left hand, then with both hands.

Drill XXV

Rhythms Formed by Using a Dot

A dot extends the value of a note one half. The following effect is always expressed with a dot; except over the bar or between the second and third pulses in quadruple meter:

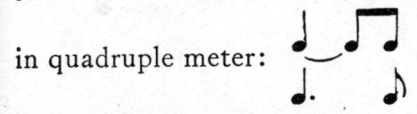

1. Recite the following word several times, visualizing the given notation:

Mary, Mary

Repeat in the following manner, feeling the subdivision into two:

Ma- -ry

It is necessary in singing and in playing the violin to stress the second pulse, which is not sounded, by a slight crescendo. It is not possible to make this crescendo upon the piano. If a slight pressure is given to the held note at the time of the second pulse the last eighth-note will be properly relaxed as the subdivision of that pulse.

2. Play the following exercise counting aloud, first with the right hand, then with the left hand, then with both hands:

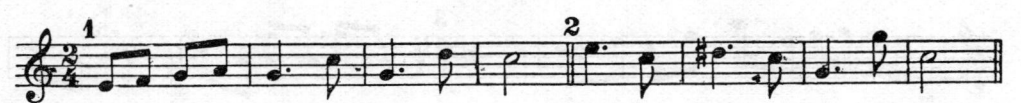

3. Play the following melodies, keeping strict time and counting aloud:

4. Play the following piano composition:

Brahms

Drill XXVI

The ♩.♪

1. Play the following exercise counting aloud, first with the right hand, then with the left hand, then with both hands:

This rhythmic figure is often carelessly played as part of a triplet  instead of four sixteenths. This can be corrected by mentally carrying the subdivision of the pulse into four. Only in a composition of the classical period, where the prevailing rhythmic subdivision has been into three, should this figure be played as part of a triplet.

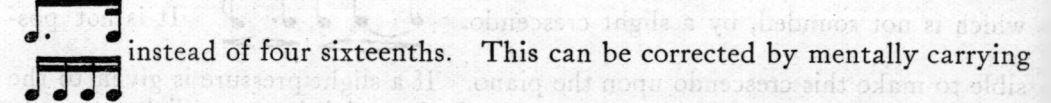

2. Play the following melodies, keeping strict time and counting aloud:

RHYTHM IN MUSIC

3. Play the following piano composition:

Scherzo

Drill XXVII

The ♪♩♪ in 6/8 Time

1. Play the following exercise counting aloud, first with the right hand, then with the left hand, then with both hands:

2. Play the following melodies, keeping strict time and counting aloud:

3. Play the following piano composition:

Doloroso

Drill XXVIII

The ♩.♫ in 6/8 Time

1. Play the following exercises counting aloud, first with the right hand, then with the left hand, then with both hands:

2. Play the following melodies, keeping strict time counting:

RHYTHM IN MUSIC

3. Play the following piano composition:

Beethoven

Drill XXIX
Thirty-Second Notes

1. Practice the following exercises, beating time and singing in a major scale as illustrated on page 40.

In a slow tempo it is necessary to subdivide the beat. The arm movement in duple meter is:

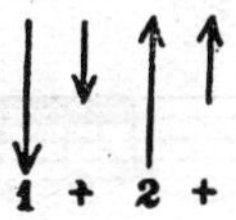

Lento

2. Play the above exercises in a major scale, counting aloud, first with the right hand, then with the left hand, then with both hands. In counting subdivided pulses it is customary to say "one and, two and."

THE TIE
Drill XXX
The Tie in Two-Pulse Meter

The instructions for playing the dotted-note given on page 41 apply to the tie. While holding the tied note, mentally subdivide the pulse into two or four if the following figure is one of four notes; into three if the following figure is a triplet.

1. Play the following exercise, counting aloud, first with the right hand, then with the left hand, then with both hands:

2. Play the following melodies, keeping strict time and counting aloud:

RHYTHM IN MUSIC 47

3. Play the following piano composition:

Drill XXXI

The Tie in Three- and Four-Pulse Meter

1. Practice the following exercises, beating time and singing in the major scale as illustrated on page 40:

Drill XXXII
The Tie in 6/8 Time

1. Play the following exercises, counting aloud, first with the right hand, then with the left hand, then with both hands:

2. Play the following melodies, keeping strict time and counting aloud:

3. Play the following piano composition:

Andante

IRREGULAR RHYTHMS
Drill XXXIII
Irregular Rhythms in Two-, Three-, Four- and Six-Pulse Meters

In performing irregular rhythms there is danger of over-stressing the longer notes and giving the audience the impression that the rhythm is regular or that there is no rhythm. The long note will stand out because it is held longer than the others. In addition, the sudden stopping of the motion causes a feeling of stress. Since the auditor as well as the performer is delighted with any rhythmic irregularity, care must be taken to make him conscious of this irregularity. This can be done only by carefully preserving the stress on the first pulse of each measure. If you wish the line, "Land of the brave, land of the free," to read with the accent on "brave" and "free," the rhythmic setting would be

$\frac{2}{4}$ ♫ ♩ ♫ ♩ If the word "land" is to be stressed, the setting would be $\frac{2}{4}$ ♫ ♩ ♫ ♩ It is apparent that in the last setting, unless care is exercised, too much stress will be given the longer notes and it will sound as if the metric accent fell upon the words "brave" and "free." It is interesting that when correctly performed the stress on "land," stressed because of its position in the measure, balances that caused by the longer notes on "brave" and "free," and to the audience seems to be about equal.

1. Play the following exercises, counting aloud, first with the right hand, then with the left hand, then with both hands. Relax after the first pulse of each measure:

2. Play the following melodies, keeping strict time and counting aloud:

3. Play the following piano composition:

Andante

SYNCOPATED RHYTHM
Drill XXXIV
Syncopated Rhythm in Two-, Three- and Four-Pulse Meters

In performing syncopated rhythms the same care must be exercised as in the case of irregular rhythms, that the metric accent and pulse be preserved.

1. Play the following exercises, counting aloud, first with the right hand, then with the left hand, then with both hands:

2. Play the following melodies, keeping strict time and counting aloud:

3. Play the following piano composition:

Larghetto

espressivo

Drill XXXV

Syncopated Rhythm in 6/8 Time

A syncopated 6/8 measure, as in the following exercise, is often printed with a quarter-note in place of the tied eighths. This is misleading, as the performer is apt to play the three quarter-notes as a measure in 3/4 time. The second pulse of the measure falls on the second tied eighth. To preserve the feeling of two pulses in the measure and to perform the last quarter-note with proper relaxation, give added pressure to the second eighth-note.

1. Play the following exercise, counting aloud, first with the right hand, then with the left hand, then with both hands:

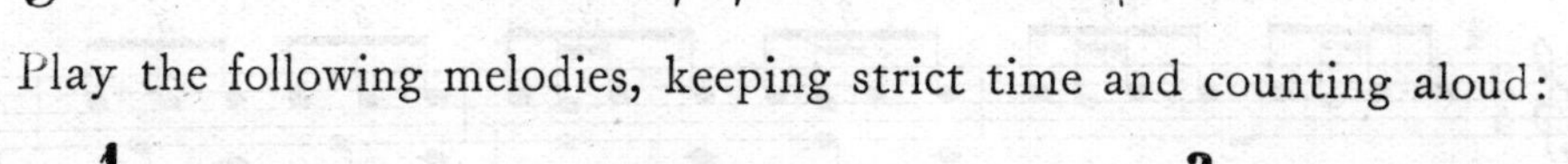

2. Play the following melodies, keeping strict time and counting aloud:

3. Play the following piano composition:

Moderato

CROSS RHYTHM

Drill XXXVI

Two against Three

The frequency with which one meets the cross rhythm two against three, makes it imperative to perform these rhythms without thought. The approximate proportion is:

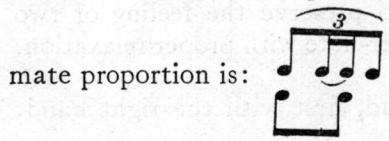

1. Practice the following exercise counting "one, two and three" for the triplet, and bringing the second eighth-note of the two-note figure on the "and."

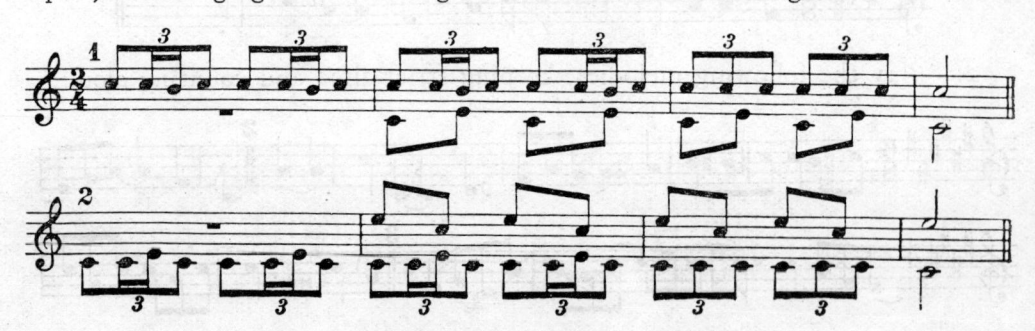

2. Play the following piano composition:

Drill XXXVII

Three against Four

In playing three against four, the second note of the triplet falls just after the second sixteenth-note; the third note just before the last sixteenth-note. An exact mathematical subdivision is:

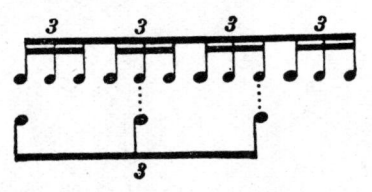

1. Practice the following exercises:

54 RHYTHM IN MUSIC

2. Play the following piano composition:

GEORGE A. WEDGE'S

EAR-TRAINING AND SIGHT-SINGING

ADVANCED EAR-TRAINING AND SIGHT-SINGING

Price, each, $2.50

COMMENT
By Four Famous Educators

"I consider Wedge's 'Ear-Training and Sight-Singing' one of the most valuable contributions to the study of these subjects as well as for Elementary Theory, that has been made in the past twenty-five years. The second volume, now available, is, if anything, even more valuable, as it covers ground practically unexplored hitherto. Those who have mastered the contents of these two books will have laid a foundation for thorough musicianship which is unshakeable and, till now, very rare."—*FRANK DAMROSCH*

"I regard the contents of these books as being, without exception, the most thorough, extensive and practical presentation of working principles, together with ample priceless material, I have ever seen."
—*THOMAS TAPPER*

"The statements are simple, but fully grounded; and the material is carefully graded, and so comprehensive as to include every detail of theory and (very especially) of *practice*, which is the strong foundation a thorough musical education absolutely requires."—*PERCY GOETSCHIUS*

"I am glad to speak in the most enthusiastic terms of the two books on sight-singing by Mr. George A. Wedge. They not only fill a long-felt want, but they fill it better than I thought possible."—*HERBERT WITHERSPOON*

G. SCHIRMER INC.   NEW YORK

A 685

Keyboard Harmony

A Practical Application of Music Theory Including the Study of Melody Harmonization, Broken Chords and Arpeggios, Transposition, Modulation and Improvisation

By **GEORGE A. WEDGE**

MUSIC THEORY is a study which has become essential to the fully equipped musician, and which, in consequence, most pupils take up as a part of their proper musical education. It is generally followed as a separate subject from the pupil's chosen instrument or particular field; very few realize its far-reaching application and value.

This book is an endeavor to show the teachers and pupils of piano how to apply, at the keyboard, each theoretic point and to give exercises for practice.

Price $2.50
(In U. S. A.)

G. Schirmer, Inc.

3 East 43rd Street   New York

A 686